YUCATAN
AND THE MAYA CIVILIZATION

TEXT: **M. WIESENTHAL**
LAYOUT: J. OPISSO
PHOTOGRAPHS: F. MONFORT

1st. Edition, July 1978
I.S.B.N.
84-7424-017-4

GEOCOLOR® S.A.

The white city *of Mérida*

Mérida Cathedral in the Main Square

The Main Square. The Municipal Square

YUCATAN

The Yucatan peninsula, stretching from the Gulf of Mexico to the Caribbean is a land inhabited by the gods, for in its sacred cities the ancient Mayas worshipped the Rain god and in its great temples and ceremonial centres the mysteries of the cosmos were studied and sacrificial rites carried out.
The Mayas called it the *Country of the Turkey and the Deer,* land of milk and honey, generous in its harvests, filled with powerful animals and colourful birds. Its present name of *Yucatan* comes from a misunderstanding. In the Maya language, *Ci-u-than* means "we don't understand each other". And this was what the inhabitants of the coast replied to the first conquistadors who landed on the beaches of Yucatan; but the name became fixed forever in the geography of the New World.
The classical history of Yucatan began around the year 600 B.C. when the Mayas from the Pacific settled in the peninsula. From the X century they built great cities and the famous Mayapan League was created, a confederation uniting the cities of Chichen-Itza, Uxmal and Mayapan. During the two centuries the *Mayapan League* lasted, Chichen-Itza

The Government Palace

*The spires of the
Cathedral*

*Inside the Government
Palace*

Mérida
Cathedral

was the most important city in the north of the peninsula. But soon serious differences arose among the members of the confederation which helped the Spaniards in their conquest of the region. After the fall of the Aztec Empire in 1521, the Spaniards began to conquer Yucatan. Initially repulsed by this proud independent people, the conquistadors began a war of attrition. They constructed new cities among the ruins of the Maya temples, sent their missionaries to ensure the spiritual conversion of the defeated peoples, and created a new network of roads through the jungle.

Their advance was slow and difficult, but the Spanish influence was to last forever in the Maya culture of Yucatan.
The Mayas often tried to regain their independence. In 1652 there was an indian uprising that cost the governor his life; in 1840 Colonel Torrens proclaimed Yucatan independent, and in 1848 a further indian uprising broke out during the so-called Guerra de las Castas (Caste War). The peninsula's geographical location and the lack of communication with the rest of Mexico favoured these separatist movements, but the situation was to change

The House of Montejo

Entrance to the Centenario Park

A fountain in the Las Américas Park

Acoustic shell in the Las Américas Park

The José Martí Library

Monument to the Motherland

Calash with Yucatán lady mestizo as passenger

Statue to the Mother

Statue to the Boy Heroes

Monument to general
Manuel Cepeda Peraza

Statue to Justo Sierra

Statue to Don Benito Juárez

Saint Christopher

radically after the 1910-1920 revolution with an improvement in the social status of the peasants and the introduction of new technological progress. Nowadays, Yucatan is one of Mexico's most outstanding tourist centres with modern agriculture, open to all types of cultural influences and in communication with the rest of the world.

THE MAYAS

The splendour and the fall of the Maya peoples is one of archaeology's great enigmas. A refined culture developed in the space of a few centuries and then disappeared, absorbed by the Spanish conquest, scarcely leaving any trace of its first steps in history. Its hieroglyphic writing tells us nothing of its past, and the best witnesses of its history that we have are from the oral tradition or the pen of Spanish missionaries. The first Maya cities suddenly disappeared from history, swallowed up by the jungle until around the year 1000 A:D. a great rebirth of the cities of Yucatan was brought about.

The Hermitage of Santa Isabel or Our Lady of the Good Journey

Saint John the Baptist

Minor Order - Church of Jesus

The parish church of Santiago (St. James)

The chapel of la Candelaria

The State Archaeological Museum in the Paseo Montejo

Views of the rooms containing Maya art in the Archaeology Museum

A courtyard and fountain in Mérida

Under the influence of other Meso-american peoples such as the Toltecs, the Mayas of Yucatan created a new culture and a true revolution in art forms with the generalized use of columns, geometrical decoration and buildings set up in large spaces. Due to trading contacts, many luxury objects from other Meso-american regions appeared in Yucatan,- precious stones, vessels made from onyx and rock crystal, obsidian knives... The rebirth of Maya art is characterized by the predominance of the warrior caste as opposed to the priests. The military orders of *Tiger Knights* and *Eagle Knights* were created probably having their origin in solar mythology,-

Yucatan University

Hotel Montejo Palace

Hotel Mérida

the rising sun being an eagle and the setting sun
a tiger disappearing into the shadows.
The Mayas created a calendar which was used for
establishing the agricultural cycle and prophecies.
Some of their temples were used for the cult of
astronomy and the study of weather cycles.
A series of codices has reached us containing
religious or scientific texts of great interest. We also
know some Maya songs collected in the Book of the
Canticles of Dzibalche, but the music to accompany
these prayers is unknown.

> *Espiador, espiador de los árboles,*
> *a uno, a dos*
> *vamos a cazar a orillas de la arboleda*
> *en danza ligera hasta tres.*

The Maya cities of the Yucatan peninsula were
independent but united in their language, religion
and similar political institutions. At the head of

Folklore dances from Yucatan

each city was the *Halach Uinic,* or local chief whose position was inherited from father to son. Religious organization was headed by the great priest, the *Ahuacan* or Lord Serpent. The priests and divines had the exclusive right to scientific knowledge. And at the base of this hierarchy were the people, the *Macehualob,* the real makers of the temples and cities; it was they who cut stones, felled trees, sculpted statues and who carried the weight of the country on their shoulders in the form of taxes.
On the lowest social level were the slaves who were often used for human sacrifice.
The features of present day Maya people still remind us of those sculpted by ancient artists. The average

height of a Maya man was 1 metre 55 cms. They had a braquicephalic cranium and flattened their children's heads so they could carry burdens better. They dressed their straight black hair in a plait and the men adorned their heads with a mirror in the shape of a disk. The women did not use this sort of decoration and when they wished to insult a

deceived husband they said "his wife had put the mirror in her own hair". The most typical feature of the Maya physiognomy is the pronounced Mongolian fold of the eyes. They considered it a distinction to have a squint, like Itzamna, the god of the heavens.

The men were dressed in a loin cloth and according

The Bull-ring - Taunting the bull

The Bull-ring - Preparing for the kill

Progreso. The quaysides at Mérida

The Progreso Beach - Yucatán

A sheltered port at Progreso - Yucatan

*The San Juan
archway*

*DZIBILCHALTUN.
The temple of
the Seven
Dolls.*

CHICHEN ITZA. The pyramid of El Castillo (The Castle) taken from the Temple of the Warriors. In the foreground is an XI century pillar in the shape of a snake.

to weather conditions, covered their shoulders with a *poncho* which was also used as a blanket for sleeping. The women wore an underskirt and a sort of shirt.

They lived in wicker houses built on a stone base covered with a straw roof. The inside was divided into two rooms —the kitchen and the bedroom. The entrance was never closed with doors; visitors announced their presence by pulling a rope to which several small bells were fastened. Their staple diet was maize, and when the peasants went out to their fields at dawn they took with them several balls of ground maize for food. When they came back in the afternoon they went to the public baths and had their main meal,- more than twenty large sized maize omlettes. But besides this cereal which constituted the basis of their diet, they grew other productos too,- the pepper *(aji* or *chili),* the sweet potatoe, the manioc, avocado pear, and cocoa for making chocolate. Maya children chewed rubber from the chicle tree.

But the great agricultural problem in Yucatan was one of drought. As the peninsula is largely composed of limestone, the rain water reached

The Pelota Game at Chichen Itza measuring
93 by 34 metress

down to the subsoil. So, in many cities large tanks or deposits were built to keep water in during these disastrous droughts. This would explain their worship of the Rain god and their offerings of living sacrifice to this terrible deity.

THE CITIES OF YUCATAN

The great Maya cities were abandoned after the Spanish conquest, but the old cultural tradition of the conquered people was perpetuated in the architecture of the colonial cities.
The Spaniards, however, contributed some elements to Maya architecture which were hitherto unknown such as the archway and iron grills on the windows. A normal house in Yucatan still has much of the precolumbine period. The majority of the buildings are oval with a cane roof held up by beams. The furniture consists merely of a few chairs, a table and hammocks used for sleeping.

MERIDA

Merida, known as the White City for the beauty and cleanliness of its streets is the commercial centre of the whole peninsula. Surrounded by the most

CHICHEN ITZA. Temple of the Warriors or the Temple of the Thousand Columns (there are only 400)

*The Pelota Game,
The Castle and Temple
of the Jaguars*

CHICHEN ITZA

El Caracol *(the snail)*
at Chicen Itza which
was used as an
observatory

The head of a serpent Chac-Mool *and standard bearer, also the Castle of CHICHEN ITZA in the background*

The head of a plumed serpent, with the Temple of the Jaguars in the background.

CHICHEN ITZA. The Temple of the Jaguars

CHICHEN ITZA. The House of the Nuns

Columns with bas-reliefs
from the Temple of the
Warriors at *CHICHEN
ITZA*

Chac-Mool *from the
Temple of the Warriors
CHICHEN ITZA*

*CHICHEN ITZA. The
Platform of the Tigers*

A sacred water tank

CHICHEN ITZA.
Tzompantli *or Platform
of Skulls*

The Castle

CHICHEN ITZA.
The Church

CHICHEN ITZA. *The
Pelota Game*

CHICHEN ITZA

important archaeological centres of Yucatan, it is a fine starting point for discovering the country. Nights in Merida are famous for their mildness. During the day, life in Merida revolves round the cool oasis of the Zocalo Square or around the main market place. Few sights are more evocative than this market where we can see the old rites of indian trading. Men with ancient mysterious faces, crouching amid mounds of multicoloured clothes, straw hats, sweet-smelling fruit, strong spices... In the popular restaurants *pibil* chicken is served, a typical dish consisting of slices of meat. But Merida's magic hour begins at sundown when its houses and streets are silhouetted in the shadows or in the moonlight; when the dripping water of the fountains sings in the courtyards, when a horse-drawn carriage crosses a silent square, when the smell of tropical flowers brings perfume, like incense, to the narrow streets the traveller strolls along.

Merida was founded on January 6th 1542 by Don Francisco de Montejo, on the same site as the former Maya city of *T'ho* had stood. The old house of the founder of the city with its magnificent plateresque style facade is still standing in the *Plaza del Zócalo.*

CHICHEN ITZA

Statue of the Jaguar

The Jaguar. A throne in the Castle incrusted with jade and with teeth made out of flint

CHAC-MOOL *in the interior Temple of* El Castillo

The capital has preserved its lovely ecclesiastical buildings from the period of Spanish domination. The cathedral- the largest place of worship in the whole Yucatan peninsula, was built in 1561. The church of San Cristobalis a perfect example of primitive Spanish architecture and the fortress with its surrounding walls gives it an impregnable, almost military air. Among the colonial style religious buildings, of special note is the white building of the *Museo de la Ermita,* a primaeval, peasant-like structure, surrounded by lovely gardens containing some precolombine remains. Also outstanding for its Moorish influence is the church of San Juan with arcades of evident Arab styling.

In the *Plaza del Zócalo* itself is the Municipal Palace with its slender tower and impressive facade made up of two arched galleries.
The favourite avenue of the inhabitants of Merida is of course the *Paseo Montejo,* flanked by old palaces such as *Palacio Cantón,* the former governor's residence, now made into a library and archaeological museum. At one end of this avenue, a grandiose monument of Maya inspiration has been built, designed by the Colombian Romulo Rozo, evoking the history of Mexico.
But Mexico is above all an open city, with green spaces, born in the middle of a natural oasis. Its fine gardens- the *Parque del Centenario,* the *Parque de*

The Castle of CHICHEN ITZA.

The Sacred Water Tank

las Américas, the *Parque Juárez,* offer the city dweller innumerable corners in which he can either meditate or chat, or take a stroll.

The warmth and gaiety of the people of Merida is shown in the healthy optimism of the carnival celebrated each year on different dates lasting for five days. The colourful masks and allegorical floats overflow onto the streets and animate the popular dances.

THE OLD TOWNS OF YUCATAN

The Yucatan peninsula is a land of legends. Its coast

Hotel "Lapalapa" at Uxmal

A general view of the ancient ruins at Uxmal

UXMAL. The Nuns' Quadrangle

gave shelter, time ago, to the Spanish galleons with their cargo of gold when they had to take refuge from the hurricanes in the Caribbean. It is a land full of contrasts, where rain comes after draught, the jungle succeeds the savannah, and cocoa plantations are not far from sandy deserts. Hidden in the safe waters of its bay is Campeche, the old fortified town where Spanish sailors took refuge. The walls of Campeche were built in the XVI century to defend the town against attacks from pirates. Its cathedral and churches jealously guard the memory of the colonial period. Campeche is famous for its festivities; the carnival, the feast of San Roman in September, and the feast of San Francisco in October. All its coastline, up to Ciudad del Carmen is a real paradise for fishermen and those fond of tropical beaches.

Half way between Merida and the Caribbean coast is the old colonial city of Valladolid, built near to a *cenote* that the Mayas used as a cistern or water deposit. These *cenotes* were formed by the crumbling of the earth's crust in places where a subterranean current of water flowed. The Mayas worshipped these as sacred places.

THE COAST AND ITS BEACHES

The entire coastline of Yucatan is fringed with lovely beaches with fine white sand, shaded by luxuriant vegetation. Some of them, such as Campeche, Progreso, or Ciudad del Carmen, belong to the Gulf of Mexico; others, such as Cozumel, Mujeres Island, Caucun, Akumal, etc. are on the Caribbean. All these beaches are completely unspoilt, with underwater

Uxmal

Uxmal. A panoramic view of the Nun's Courtyard

Uxmal. The Nun's Courtyard, in the Centre the Temple of Venus.

gardens or coral reefs as in Akumal and Xel ha. In the lagoon at Can cun an enormous tourist complex has been built which has nothing to envy of the famous beaches at Acapulco. At a cost of almost 100 million dollars, hotels, sports centres, residential colonies, clubs, night clubs and other places of entertainment have been built. On the Caribbean coast, in the Quintana Roo territory,- thus named in memory of a poet of the Independence-, there is a long succession of virgin beaches - an ecological paradise inhabited by innumerable species of fish and birds where there are still many unexplored places to be found.

THE ISLANDS OF COZUMEL AND MUJERES

The islands of Yucatan, joined to the peninsula by fast means of communication, have become first-rate tourist centres.
The island of Cozumel in the Caribbean is of interest archaeologically and has come charming fishing villages. The capital of Cozumel, San Miguel, is a sleepy white village on the sea shore, where Spanish boats have taken refuge in its old port ever since the XVI century. All its streets and avenues lead

Uxmal. Entrance to the Nuns' Courtyard

to the sea. The San Francisco beach, the most famous on the island, is protected by a cliff from tides and storms.

The island of Mujeres is smaller and attracts a younger type of tourist, nature lovers and sea sports enthusiasts. Its most famous beach, los Cocoteros, has shallow waters and a delightful tropical atmosphere.

IMPORTANT ARCHAEOLOGICAL CENTRES

There are more than 50,000 archaeological centres in Yucatan preserving the traces of Maya history. The immense temple-cities of the Mayas were at the same time religious and civic centres. Legions of specialized workmen toiled in the construction of these enormous buildings. They used lime mortar and cut the blocks of stone with stone axes. Their cities were so numerous and large that a Spanish missionary described them saying —"The whole country looked like one city". Many of these ruins have been excavated and studied, but there are still many remains hidden in the jungle and the tropical forests.

Uxmal. The western building on the Nuns' Quadrangle

Uxmal. The Governor's Palace

Two details of the god Chac *(the rain god)*

MAYAPAN

Though the city of Mayapan is not as important archaeologically as other religious centres, it is the only Maya capital which is really known. Founded towards the end of the X century it extended its influence over the majority of the cities is Yucatan. Excavations have revealed a walled precinct and many platforms used as a base for temples and dwellings. The inhabitants paid no taxes and shared their goods according to a strict community organization. The city instigated a political confederation with Chichen Itza and Uxmal which is known by the name of the *Mayapan League.* But their prosperity ended suddenly, seventy five years before the arrival of the Spaniards, because of internal dissention provoked by fighting between rival dynasties.

CHICHEN ITZA

Chichen Itza was the largest of the Maya cities in the Yucatan. According to tradition it was founded three times during the years 432, 964 and 1,194

Uxmal. Pyramid of the Deviner

A.D. Its great pyramid rises up in the middle of a vast plain where two sacred wells had existed in earlier times.

The real rebirth of Maya art in Chichen Itza began about the year 1000 when the Itzaes emigrated to this region of the Yucatan. It is not known where these invaders actually came from, but in some way they had been in contact with the Toltec people living in the Mexican metropolis of Tula. An old cycle of legends tells the story of the Toltec hero *Quetzalcóatl* who went into exile having been expelled from his own country. More than 1,500 kilometres separate Tula —the former Toltec metropolis— from the Maya city of Chichen Itza; jungles, deserts, and enemy tribes make any communication even more difficult. However, it is obvious that the influence of Tula and the men of *Quetzalcóatl* reached Yucatan. This influence of the central Mexican peoples can be detected in all the buildings in the Maya capital. The pyramid called *Castillo* is the most important construction in Chichen Itza. It was given this name by the Spaniards because they thought it to be a fortress. It was actually dedicated to the cult of *Kukulcán*

Uxmal. Pyramid of the Deviner

Uxmal. Masks of the rain god Chac

*Uxmal. Building on the north side of the Nuns'
Quadrangle, with the Temple of Venus in the foreground*

(a Maya translation of *Quetzalcóatl*) and built in accordance with the mysterious symbols of the astronomical and solar rites; its steps are divided into four series consisting of 91 steps each, which when added to those on the top platform comes to 365 - the number of days in the year. The pyramid is made up of eighteen parts (nine storeys divided by a central staircase corresponding to the number of months in the Maya calendar). On the top platforms is a great domed temple with pillars representing plumed serpents.

Inside this pyramid archaeologists discovered another older temple also evidencing Toltec influence. A secret staircase gave access to the throne room of the *Red Jaguar* where stood the figure of a jaguar with its jaws open, adorned with jade disks.

One of the most characteristic buildings in Chichen Itza is the so-called *Pelota Game.* This is a precinct closed in by two vertical walls. The object of the game,- in a way rather similar to present day basket ball,- was to pass the ball through the stone rings placed on the wall seven metres from the ground. The winners were rewarded with the jewels,

Uxmal. Parts of the frieze in the western building of the Nuns' Quadrangle

Uxmal. Detail from the masks of Chac *on the central door of the eastern building on the Nuns' Quadrangle*

adornments and clothes of the spectators: the losers were probably put to death.

Toltec influence is especially evident in the Warriors' Temple. Its decoration contains many elements that are characteristic of Tula architecture,- jaguars, plumed snakes, eagles, and the famous colonnade holding up interlaced wooden beams. In this building is the recumbent sculpture of *Chac-Mool* with the tray in her hands on which the still warm hearts of victims were placed. There is a large open courtyard in front of the temple which the Spaniards called *The Courtyard of the Thousand Columns;* there are really not even four hundred of them but they doubtless give the impression of more. Nearby is a courtyard surrounded by pillars which was perhaps covered by palm leaves and used as a market. One of the most unusual features of Maya culture is their study of astronomy. Different observatories were built by the Mayas for research

into astronomical phenomena. In Chichen Itza are the ruins of a tower destined for use in the observation of the heavens, By means of openings in the upper part, certain points of astronomical observation could be fixed; one of the windows looked to the geographic South, and the sunset could be observed through the others during the vernal and autumnal equinoxes, also the setting of the moon on the same dates. By these means, the Mayas were able to divide time exactly, in accordance with lunar cycles; they were able to calculate fairly accurately the period of revolution of Venus and made a calendar that influenced other Mesoamerican peoples. By scrutinizing the mysteries of the calendar, they made their prophesies according to their apocalyptic belief in the future end of the world. Water was, as has been stated, one of the great problems of Maya agriculture. They worshipped the Rain god and

The Loltun Caves

*Water Tank at the
entrance to Valladolid.*

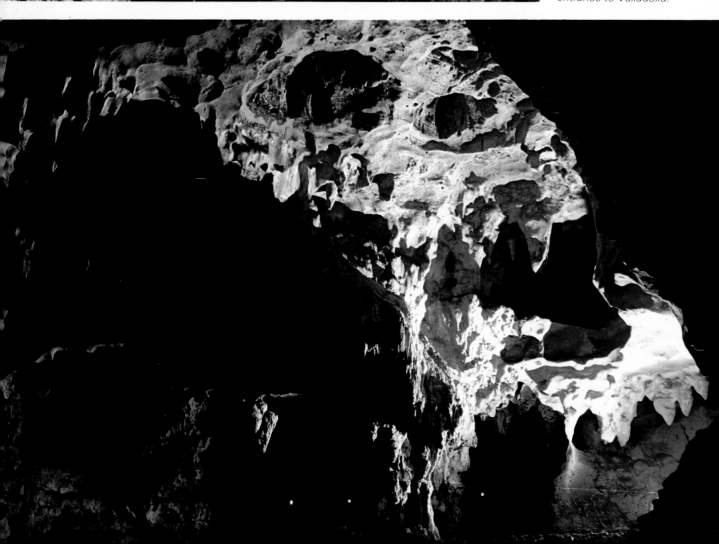

Mayapan

celebrated his religious rites close by the great *cenotes* or cisterns. In Chichen Itza are two of these water deposits , one for practical use and the other the sacred *cenote* of old Chichen. The latter measured 60 metres in circumference, 20 metres up to the level of the water, 16 metres of water and 3 metres of mud in the bottom.
Archaeological exploration has revealed that it was used for human sacrifice.
A few kilometres from Chichen Itza on the road to Valladolid, we come upon one of the sancturies where this profound worship of water developed by the Maya civilization is best expressed,- the

Grotto of Balancanche. This sacred Maya sanctuary remained miraculously closed for a thousand years until 1959 when a guide by chance leaned against a wall and penetrated into the cave. Through a natural tunnel along which one has to go almost on all fours, it is possible to reach a chamber covered with stalactites and stalagmites. The formation of the rock is similar in shape to an enormous ceiba, the sacred Maya tree. Amid this damp growth of stalactites, hundreds of objects left there as offerings to the Rain god were found. This natural temple, hidden and difficult to reach, was probably only known about by the priests and

Kabah - A general view. In the background to the left is House II

Kabah - Codz Poop or the Palace of the Masks.

Kabah - A Maya archway

Kabah

Kabah

The Temple of the Pillars

The Facade of Codz Poop, *masks of the god* Chac

high civic dignitaries.

Another of the curious characteristic rites of Yucatan is the phallic cult, related to sexuality and the fecundation of the earth by sowing. We have found one of these temples decorated with phallic symbols of Toltec derivation in Chichen Itza.

The ruins of Chichen Itza are full of enigmas, some of them coming from the very names that the Spaniards gave to these strange buildings whose foundation was unknown. Who lived in this great palace that the conquistadors called the Casa de las Monjas? What was the meaning of the red hands painted on the roof of the *Akad-Dzib* or *Temple of the unknown writing?* Does the steam bath taken by the priests before their prayers have some ritualistic significance? We can still visit one of these steam baths near to the *Square of a Thousand Columns,* with its low roof where steam was produced by

The Labna Archway

Labna. The Maya Archway

throwing water onto hot stones.
The decadence of Chichen Itza came about suddenly, during the Spanish conquest. Mysterious iguanas now slumer like pieces of sculpture on its ruins, inviting the traveller to meditate deeply on the history of this lost people.

UXMAL

The ruins of Uxmal are some 65 kilometres from the city of Merida. Along with Chichen Itza and Mayapan

Sayil. The Palace

The Palace

Labna. The Puuc *style Palace*

it made up the famous confederation known by the name of the *Mayapan League,* but as opposed to the other ceremonial centres, it evidences less influence from the central Mexican cultures. Although it was not a large city, it contains the purest architectural samples of the Maya style. The city is located in the middle of a large hilly plain. This region is known as *Puuc,* and the same word is applied to its peculiar architectural style which is different from the *chenes* style characteristic of the rest of the peninsula.

All the Maya cities of the *Puuc* region were joined together by so-called *sacbeob* or *sacred roadways.* The first Spaniards to arrive in the country spoke of these roads and called them "beautiful, broad and flat". However, the Mayas did not use beasts of burden and carried everything on their backs. Only the chieftains were carried about in large litters decorated with plumes.

The *Puuc* region is dry and arid; but the inhabitants of Uxmal solved the problem of their water supply by building artificial cisterns called *chultunes.* Rain water was collected in declivities in the ground previously lined with mortar; this was a prodigious feat of engineering showing the technical ability of these people. The *Wizard's Pyramid,* also known as the *Divine's Pyramid* dominated the whole city with its impressive oval structure. A lovely legend is attached to this building. They say an old sorcerer incubated a child in an egg. The child grew, gifted with many talents until be became chief citizen, and one of his feats was to have built the Great Pyramid in only one night. The truth is that this building, as shown by archaeological excavations, was built in successive stages throughout 300 years. The oldest section which is the base of the present

Temple of the Three Masks

pyramid was decorated with masks and architectural elements somewhat related to the art of Teotihuacan. It was there where the famous sculpture of the Queen of Uxmal was found which today is in the Mexico City National Anthropological Museum. It is a serpent's head with the likeness of a priest coming out of its jaws. The other sections of the pyramid were built at a later date, on top of the preceding ones, until they reached a height of 35 metres. The Governor's Palace, the administrative centre of Uxmal, is one of the most noteworthy and best proportioned in all Maya art. Built on three terraces overlooking a wide plain the lower part of the facade is smooth, while the upper part is covered with and ornamental stone frieze whose stones are joined with such precision that they appear to be a mosaic. Probably this is the culmination of all precolumbine art,

in its sense of rhythm and the harmonious distribution of its elements.

Behind the Wizard's pyramid is the *Casa de las Monjas,* so called by the Conquistadors who thought it was a convent on account of the many rooms inside it. The different rooms in the building made up a quadrangle surrounding a courtyard. The different decoration on its facades ranges from a classical sobriety to the most exuberant baroque, and even the colour of the stones is perfectly chosen to produce a wonderful effect of light and shade.

In Uxmal as well as in other cities of Yucatan, the phallic cults also had their sacred sanctuaries. In the so-called *Phallic Temple,* they probably celebrated these ceremonies related to the fertility cult. Along the roof are some phallic shapes probably used as channels to drain off the rain water. In front of the Governor's Palace stands an enormous stone phallus, broken off in the middle and not restored for reasons "of a moral nature". And in the *Casa de las Monjas* itself, in the decoration on the facade are figures of men with an abnormally large penis.

The inhabitants of Uxmal had a passion for the game of *Pok-a-tok,* similar to present day basket ball. The players wore special protection on the arms, waists, knees and heads. The old Maya chronicle of *Popol Vuh* contains a mysterious reference to the pelota game:

"Let us play pelota, said the lord of Xibalba.
Then the gentlemen caught the ball and sent it
Straight towards the ring of Hunahpu".

The only pelota game discovered in Uxmal is in a very bad state, but archaeologists have reconstructed its 40 metres long parallel walls. Also, work is continuing on the reconstruction of the Great Pyramid which was, in its time, as large as the Wizard's Pyramid and has several features of the purest decorative style of the *Puuc.*

The most characteristic element of Maya architecture is the false archway or console archway. The stones are placed in such a way that each row juts out a little above the lower one until there is only one squared stone on the upper part. At one end of the archaeological area of Uxmal, on the *sacred road* joining the capital to the nearby city of Kabah, stands a fine example of a Maya archway.

Palenque. A general view

Another one in the same style is in the *Courtyard of the Dovecots.*

The Maya have left very few written documents pertaining to their history. There only remains the information contained in their calendars and some dates written on steles. Some of these steles or commemorative stones engraved with hieroglyphics which have still not been deciphered, were found in Uxmal.

Uxmal is the city of the plumed serpent. On almost all its buildings we discover the disquieting traces of this royal symbol. This city is the purest Maya settlement in Yucatan with a characteristic concept of civic architecture,- buildings grouped in squares, dispersed, and with no apparent orientation, lacking the compact structure of the type of the Acropolis, so common in the central area. The *Puuc* architecture of Uxmal is sterner in shape and more rigid in its volumes. The mystical vision of the Mayas reduced the universe of natural shapes to elemental geometrical outlines.

KABAH

Linked to Uxmal by a sacbe or *sacred roadway* is the ancient Maya city of Kabah. At the entrance to this architectural ensemble we also find a large console archway. This town also drank rain water collected in a cistern. Its surroundings were densely populated during the XI and XII centuries.

The most characteristic building of Kabah is the

Palenque

Palenque. The Temple of the Sun and the Palace to the right

temple known as *Codz-Poop,* decorated with masks depicting *Chac* the Maya Rain god. The facade of the sanctuary was one of the most characteristic works in *Puuc* style; a veritable forest of baroque shapes with the hooked nose of the Rain god outstanding as a ornamental motif.

LABNA

Less then 10 kilometres away from Uxmal is the city of Labna, an old ceremonial centre that was probably abandoned before its final construction. Here we come upon a console archway that opens out onto a group of buildings. On the side sections of the archway is a stylized representation of a native house. It was from these humble constructions made from mud and palm leaves that Maya architecture developed. They were painted in bright colours and rested on a stone foundation. When their inhabitants died, they were buried under the floor and the house was abandoned.
Labna has an impressive palace which stands on an artificial hill and has two large cisterns for the water supply.

SAYIL

This is one of the oldest cities in the region in *Puuc* style. There are some references to its existence at the beginning of the IX century and perhaps this is why it is of such classic simplicity. The palace of Sayil with its three terraced sections, is a true monument to proportion. It lacks the exuberant decoration we find in other *Puuc* style buildings and the measured shank of its columns reminds us slightly of the sobriety of the doric Parthenon.

DZIBILCHALTUN

This city in the north of Yucatan has been only recently excavated and is perhaps one of the most

The Great Palace with
its Square Tower

Palenque. A partial view
of the ruins

Palenque. The Temple of the Sun

Palenque. The Temple of the Cross

ancient ceremonial centres of the Maya empire. Here, a *sacred avenue* has been discovered which is more than 10 metres wide. The architectural simplicity of the *Temple of the Seven Dolls* shows that the origin of the town dates back to a period previous to the cassical revolution and the influence of the central Mexican cultures. The name of the temple is derived from the small figurines, similar to dolls, found inside the building. The town was supplied with water from a *cenote* which now looks like a romantic lake covered with water plants.

EDZNA
This ancient city in the state of Campeche, underwent the influence of different cultures through the centuries.
The five storeyed pyramid at Edzna shows the influence of the *Petén, Chenes* and *Puuc* styles. The city is beautifully planned with large squares and open spaces.

TULUM
Tulum is a walled city, unique of its type, situated

Palenque. The Temple of the Count

*Palenque.
The lid of the
tomb in the
Temple of the
Inscriptions*

Palenque. The Temple of the Inscriptions. The only monument in Maya architecture which is both a pyramid and a tomb

*Palenque.
Cylindrical incense
holders with
divinities
representing* Earth,
Sun *and* Rain

*Palenque. A jade
mask and
necklaces.*

on the shores of the Caribbean, which was inhabited up to the Spanish conquest. It was the first city seen by Cortes when he sailed along the eastern coast of Yucatan. The Spanish priest Juan Díaz recounts that he saw... "three large cities two miles apart from each other. There were many stone houses... We discovered a city so large that Seville would not have seemed larger..."
The city still looks like an impregnable fortress up on a cliff with the waves beating against it, enclosed inside a solid line of walls. Five narrow gateways in the walls give access to the urban precinct.

A present day Maya story relates that in former times the city of Tulum was joined to Coba, Chichen Itza and Uxmal by a road suspended in the sky. Although the reference is only a poetic legend, it is true that Tulum was linked by road to other cities.
The fortified structure of Tulum shows that the hypothesis of the pacific nature of the Mayas is inaccurate, revealing the warlike tradition of these people who went into battle fully prepared. They attacked their enemies with slings, lances, maces, and a weapon that shot arrows, mentioned with terror by Bernal Diaz, called the *atl-atl.* Wars usually

Palenques. Temples surrounded by luxuriant vegatation

took place in the month of October, when it was not time for harvesting the maize crop. The warriors attacked en masse and if their adversaries resisted, they threw wasps' nests into the enemy ranks. Then they charged, banging drums and blowing whistles. When the chief died the war was finished. Also, as they fought according to strict ritualistic norms, they never joined battle at night. Basically, the farming instinct of these peoples was always predominant over their enthusiasm for war, as they abandoned all engagements when the time came to sow their crops. And even in 1848 during the *War of the Castes,* the indians who had laid siege to the capital, Merida, retired when the maize planting season drew near.

In the architecture of Tulum the influence of the Toltecs of central Mexico is also evident in their use of columns in the courtyards and vestibules, the image of the plumed serpent on capitals and pinnacles, etc.

But their buildings also evidence certain features peculiar to the Caribbean, such as wing-walls. The most noteworthy of Tulum's monuments is the temple of *Kukulcán* which stands on a cliff by the

Palenque.

Palenque. The small temple on the hill

Palenque. The Maya archway

sea.

In the *Temple of the Frescoes* there are some paintings in a bluish green colour on a black background depicting offerings of flowers, fruit and maize. The bluish colour was the symbol of sacrifice and was obtained by using a special clay. The importance of Tulum was based on the fact that it was one of the cities best known by the Spanish Conquistadors. Gonzalo de Guerrero was taken prisoner by the chief of Tulum and became integrated to such a degree in the Maya way of life that he declined to return to his compatriots, pierced his ears, nose and mouth, married an indian girl and was the founder of the first half caste Mexican family.

BONAMPAK

This city situated on the frountier with Guatamala is difficult to get to, and can only be reached by air. However, a visit to it is certainly worth while to see

Palenque. The Palace Courtyard with its tower

Palenque. The
Palace
Courtyard

Palenque.
Bas-relief of the
slaves

Palenque

the fine mural paintings discovered there in 1946. The city is on a hill and built round a large square. The Bonampak frescoes have revolutionized many of the concepts previously held with regard to Maya history. These murals stretching through three rooms make up a story: an attack on enemy territory, an assembly of chieftains, a trial of prisoners and a feast to celebrate the vistory. The paintings are prodigiously colourful and expressive, executed according to traditional fresco techniques, on the damp cement of a wall, the artist did a drawing and his helpers applied the colours. The colours probably had a mystical or psychological significence like those from the palette of the great painters. Black, obtained from carbon symbolized war, yellow, the colour of maize, represented food, red meant blood. The most difficult colour to make was a deep shade of purple which was extracted from a molusc *(purpura patula)* like the famous dyes the Phoenicians used for cloth. But the most characteristic colour of Bonampak is undoubtedly the "Maya blue" obtained from some type of earth in the region.

The Bonampak frescoes make up a fantastic frieze of Maya daily life; it is a window through which we can view their religious ceremonies, their sacrifices

Palenque. "Building C." Two Maya profiles in the center of a Glifo.

and customs. Hidden in the middle of the jungle, the *city of the painted walls* —the translation of its Maya name— has jealously guarded the secrets of history for centuries.

PALENQUE

The city of Palenque is submerged in the midst of tropical vegetation. For centuries it was a hidden mysterious city. Hernan Cortes passed close by it, at a distance of less than 50 kilometres without discovering it. Some indians revealed its existence in 1773 to the Spanish priest Fray Ramon Ordoñez, who attributed the foundation of the city to the mythical Atlantes. In 1786 it was visited by captain Antonio del Rio who caused great destruction in the ruins with his daring use of excavation as a military technique. These reports reached the court of Spain and were collected by some British scientists thus provoking great interest in the excavations. Palenque is one of the loveliest enclaves of Maya art due to its geographical location in the middle of a damp plain. Its building are mysteriously identified with the countryside as if they formed part of the same damp jungle nature that surrounds

Palenque.

Palenque. The Temple of the Inscriptions

them. Several groups of buildings separated by a stream of water canalized by the Mayas have been excavated.

The most important building in Palenque is the *Great Palace* with its watch tower four storeys high with an inside staircase, a unique feature in Maya architecture. The architectural style of Palenque is reminiscent of that of the Maya hovels although here they have been raised to the rank of palaces.

The *temples of the Cross, the Sun, the Inscriptions* and *the Foliated Cross* are very similar in their external structure which is that of an artificial pyramid with a building on top crowned by a decorated roof. The facades of these palaces were decorated in former times with bright colours.

The Palenque architecture is very balanced in its volumes unlike other Maya cities whose buildings were constructed according to no previously laid out plan. Windows and openings in the walls delicately lightened the aspect of these buildings. It could be said that the constructions at Palenque, having surpassed the traditional Maya fear of openings onto the outside, constituted a real architectural revolution.

The *Temple of the Inscriptions* is a singular case in Maya architecture. Under this pyramid is the hidden tomb of an important person. This secret crypt, unique in all Mesoamerican architecture, shows that the pyramid could also be used as a burial mound as it was in other ancient cultures. The death chamber was discovered in 1951 when a Mexican archaeologist lifted a stone in the temple and went down the staircase into the crypt. The passage way was covered with rubble except for a magic passage that joined the temple to the soul of the dead man. The story of the discovery of this tomb is really

Palenque

thrilling. The archaeologist Alberto Ruz Lhuillier
worked untiringly for two years to clean the rubble
from the passage way; he first found some
offerings, the a wall, and then the remains of some
sacrifices, and finally, after lifting the stone covering
the entrance, he found what was a real fairy palace.
Through the centuries, the water filtering through
the ceiling had formed a forest of stalactites in the
immense crypt where the dead man lay. The walls
were decorated with stucco reliefs and in the middle
of the chamber was an enormous block of sculpted
stone containing the sarcophagus. Under a sealed
stone they found the skeleton of the important
dignitary buried there with a mask of jade mosaic
encrusted with jewels.
The Mayas believed in immortality and in a god who

Palenque. A bend in the River Otolum

A Guayabera (shirt) from Mérida   *Typical dress of the Yucatan Lady mestizo*   *A Guayabera (shirt) from Mérida*

rewarded the good and punished the bad. Those who obeyed the religious commandments went to heaven, the place situated in the shade of the "First tree in the world" where the blessed drank their ration of cocoa. The possessions of the dead man were considered taboo and buried with him. Many nobles were cremated and their ashes kept in statuettes depicting their faces. Thus, the secret crypt at Palenque is a mysterious exception to the funeral customs of Yucatan.

Interesting fragments of sculptures have also been found in Palenque evidencing a vigorous realism. They lengthened the faces and deformed the cranium in their sculptures to give them a mystic appearance and an inner strength that reminds us of the stylized faces of El Greco. Some of the reliefs at Palenque, such as the *Mask of death* guarding the entrance to the *Temple of the Skull,* and *The priest bearing offerings* of the Palace, have no rival in the entire Maya world.

The temples, frescoes and reliefs at Palenque reflect the image of an art which had reached the limit of its possibilities, and a society that had found the mystic expression of its feelings by creating a new image of man.

FOOD

Food in the Yucatan has its roots in history. It is mentioned in the ancient Maya codices where fruit and the food of the country,- tomatoes, maize, cocoa, chillis etc. are depicted. The cuisine of the Yucatan is vigorous and strong like all Mexican cooking. The ancient Mayas were masters of the art of condimenting their food and knew of many herbs with which to season their dishes. The basis of prehispanic cooking was maize, and maize omlettes are still the most characteristic and popular food in Maya cuisine.

After the conquest, the Spaniards also contributed their rich gastronomic tradition to the specialities of the indians. From this cultural intermingling came the rich, varied cuisine of the Yucatan we know today.

One of the peninsula's most characteristic dishes is the *mucbi-pollos* or large *tamal* made with maize dough, wrapped in banana leaves, eaten as a ritual on the Day of the Dead. For dessert excellent fruit jellies are eaten or typical sweets brought to the country by Spanish missionaries.

Chocolate, highly appreciated by the Mayas, is drunk

White filling

Papadzules

Pocchue

Lime *soup*

Steak with potatoes

A venison steak

in three ways: in the French way with milk, in the Spanish which is very thick, and in the Mexican way, very thin with water added.

HANDWORK

The delicate sensitivity of the artists who decorated the ancient Maya palaces is now expressed in the popular manufactures from Yucatan. The indian market is a unique sight in its dynamism and colour. The indian works aristically in metals, pottery and agave fibre. With this fibre obtained from the leaves of the pita or agave plant they make hats, handbags and mats. With the shell of the carey tortoise they also make different hand made objects. And in cloth, the famous *guayaberas* —tropical blouses— are an example of the imaginative artistic expression of the Maya people.

A henequen plant

Cordomex

Products made from henequen

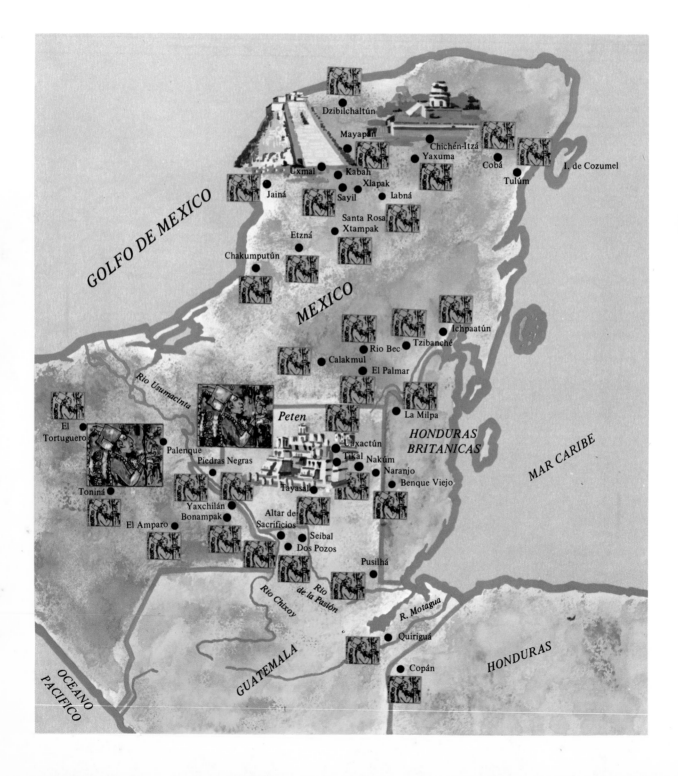

GOLFO DE MEXICO

MEXICO

Dzibilchaltún

Mayapán

Uxmal Kabah
Xlapak
Jainá Sayil Labná

Santa Rosa
Xtampak

Etzná

Chakumputún

Chichén-Itzá Yaxuma

Cobá

Tulúm

I. de Cozumel

Ichpaatún

Tzibanché

Rio Bec

Calakmul

El Palmar

La Milpa

Peten

Rio Usumacinta

El Tortuguero

Palenque
Piedras Negras

Toniná

Yaxchilán
Bonampak

El Amparo

Altar de
Sacrificios

Seibal
Dos Pozos

Uaxactún

Tikal Nakúm

Naranjo

Benque Viejo

Tayasal

Pusilhá

HONDURAS
BRITANICAS

MAR CARIBE

Rio Chixoy

Rio
de la Pasión

R. Motagua

Quiriguá

Copán

GUATEMALA

OCEANO
PACIFICO

HONDURAS

Index

Printed in Spain   GEOCOLOR®